ISBN: 979837604918

Copyright © Max de Grussa 2023

The right of Max de Grussa to be identified as the author of this work has been asserted by him in accordance with the Copyright, Designs and Patents Act 1988.

All rights reserved. No part of this publication may be reproduced, stored in a retrievable system, or transmitted in any form, or by any means (electronic, mechanical, photocopying, recording or otherwise) without the prior written permission of the author and publisher.

Amazon does not have any control over, or any responsibility for, any author or third party websites referred to in this book.

This book is sold subject to the condition that it shall not, by way of trade or otherwise, be lent, hired out, or otherwise circulated without the publisher's prior consent in any form of binding or cover other than that in which it is published and without a similar condition including this condition being imposed on the subsequent purchaser.

FOR

Angelique, Colette and Jacqueline

My three daughters whom I love and admire for not only who they are but also for what they have achieved and endured as they have progress through their lives. Hopefully they also enjoy their adventures as much as I have.

FLYING ADVENTURES

Identification patch

Flight patch
(see page 48)

Max de Grussa

Contents

Flying Adventures	4
Introduction	5
Flying Adventures	6-47
Flight Patch: Explanation	48
Confessions	49
Airfields flown From and To	50
Aircraft Description	51-86

Flying Adventures

All up I have completed 429 hours of flying as a pilot in various aircraft with every hour being a flying adventure and I absolutely loved every minute of it.

Flying is a package deal from maintaining qualifications, to the maintenance of the aircraft, to preparing the aircraft for flight after flight planning of course. I was just in that period when sophisticated electronic flight computers were developing into general aviation full 'glass' cockpits but pen, paper and charts were good to learn from the outset. Happy times and happy memories for such a fortunate fellow!

Introduction

Life has been an adventure for me. I have always seen my life as a constant supply of adventures that just seem to pop up as I cruise along exploring my environment and poking my nose into the future. A succession of life bubbles starting with childhood, teen years then young adulthood and so on. Each bubble filled with adventures.

The concept of flying has always been an exciting concept, to see what the birds see, to see earth from up there. I have a tattoo on my back of a Spitfire in the clouds with an inscription:

"I have danced with sunlit clouds"

Referring to aerobatics I was fortunate enough to carry out in a WWII Spitfire, a Slingsby T67M and my beloved RAF Bulldog trainer.

My aviation 'period' was varied, rich with interest and excitement so I have written a few snippets below for anyone interested.

This Boy's Dream

The hairs stood up on the back of my neck at sound of the Tiger Moth DH82's engine, awakening a sense of excitement within. I scanned the sky until I saw the spec on the horizon. The spec grew, as did that engine sound until the small biplane came into full view. At the age of twelve I was beside myself with excitement. A biplane this far out in the rural areas was a rare spectacle indeed. The biplane circled around my father and me while the pilot looked at the field where we had driven to for a place to land. Satisfied it was safe to land the pilot steadily banked into a turn, lined up with the field and descended gracefully to land perfectly then taxied to the utility before cutting the engine. The quietness was deafening except for the hissing and popping of the cooling engine but there she sat in all her glory, this thing of beauty waiting for me to carry out an inspection. The pilot dismounted leaving his goggles and leather helmet on the seat in the rear cockpit. While he talked to my father about the crop spraying requirements I walked to the biplane where the cooling exhaust was still crackling and hissing in disgust as it was meant to fly. She really was a thing of beauty. These heavier than air vintage machines still fascinate me to this very day.

From Perth to East Kondut

When I was six years old I moved with my family to live on a farm at East Kondut one hundred and twenty miles (180 km) northeast of Perth. It was here where the crops of wheat, oats and barley were planted and as they grew the weeds grew with them. The aerial spraying companies were contracted to spray crops with weed killer letting the crops grow without competition.

In those days of the nineteen fifties and sixties, De Havilland DH82a Tiger Moth aircraft were converted from military trainers to spray planes. Initially, it was a primary pilot trainer during World War Two (WWII) so after the war had ended they became surplus to requirements and sold for civilian use.

This tandem two-seat bi-plane trainer had the front seat replaced with a tank for the chemical spray that was applied to the field from spray booms on the lower wings.

As a boy I watched these aircraft year after year racing five feet above the crops spraying the weeds then climbing in a tight turn to repeat the spraying run back the other way until the field had been covered. It would then race away to reload and spray another field. It was the most exciting thing I had ever seen. I dreamt of being one of the daredevil pilots. The excitement and fascination with aeroplanes and flying never left me.

Bob Cooper Crop Spraying Co.

I attended primary school in Ballidu, then secondary school Tuart Hill Senior High School in Perth and finally Cunderdin Agricultural School. Cunderdin Agricultural School was located on an ex-RAAF (Royal Australian Air Force) airfield used for pilot training during WWII. The school dormitories were the old RAAF barracks and classrooms in administration buildings, we ate in the old RAAF mess. The runways were in top condition as they had been resurfaced after the war to be used in an emergency if Perth airport, for whatever reason was out of action. RAAF base Pearce, at Bullsbrook also had the Cunderdin airfield as a reserve. There was only one hanger (large buildings to house aeroplanes) left at Cunderdin as the others were sold off after WWII ended in 1945. This hanger was 'out of bounds' for us students, however … every now and then I would sneak down and even though the hanger was locked, around the side was a vent that I could squeeze through. Inside was an old disassembled de Havilland (DH83) Fox Moth that I would sit in and try to imagine what it would be like to fly.

It was at this airfield that Bob Cooper Crop Spraying Co. had its head office and at sixteen years of age I was fortunate to land a job with this company, as after seeding of crops on the family farm was completed and general farm work was quiet. My job was 'Marker' (one of two of us) that entailed holding a large red flag, starting at the edge of the paddock (field/crop) and the other guy would be at the other end of the paddock on the same side with both of us striding out forty paces, stopping while the plane flew past spraying toxic chemicals to kill the weeds. The fact that both of us were sprayed along with the weeds was irrelevant. No health and safety in those days. I did develop severe asthma though as no breathing filter masks. My jeans were saturated with this toxic spray at the end of each day with a consequence of a series of skin problems and all the hair fell off my legs with my thighs remaining bald with a red rash for many years.

However, the upside was I earnt six hundred pound ($1,200) equivalent to $11,500 2022, and bought a brand new Austin Mini Minor 850.

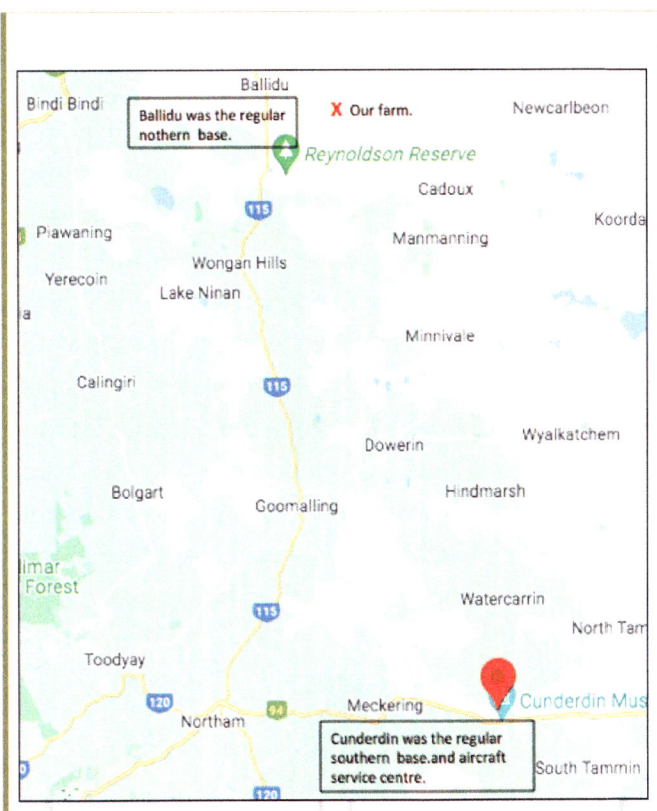

This map shows the approximate area that Bob Cooper Crop Spraying Co. was operating in using a DH82a Tiger Moth biplane where I was employed as a field marker.

While I was working with the crop spraying team (Pilot: Ben Ward; Truck Driver: Keith ?; Markers: Chris Leahy & Max de Grussa.) I was constantly infatuated with the biplane and had my first flight 'ON' this spray plane. Yes ON the plane. On several occasions when we finished spraying a paddock we needed to move to the next paddock. Normally we drove in a company utility but several times because the next field was not far away and there wasn't much daylight left so Ben our pilot got me to sit on front edge of the lower wing holding onto the outer strut with legs dangling over the front edge of the wing with Chris on the other wing. Ben then flew the plane at low level to the next field dropping us off to take our positions to mark the field. After spraying he flew us back to the utility. No thought of health and safely just needed to get the job done.

Sat here holding strut

How thrilling sitting on the wing holding the vertical strut with Chris on the other side to balance the aeroplane in flight. One occasion Ben had to ferry me to pick up the utility so I had to stand on the wing walkway next to where the pilot sat and hold onto the inner strut. My rather less terrifying flying experience was my first 'real' flight sitting in the front tandem seat in a DH95 Moth Minor. (Flown from the rear)

That's Ben and me in the Moth Minor – **NOT**. Just an example of the plane!!

It was only a four to five month season but the pay was great. It also helped to consolidate my love of aeroplanes and the prospect of becoming a pilot.

Pre-Flying Lessons

Nothing much happened after those early days as like everyone else I got caught up with life, work, wife and family, which were great adventures in itself, another story. Although my interest in flying didn't wane at all, the opportunities to fly were few and far between. I had a trip in a Cessna 172 with a friend from Wongan Hills; there was a flight in a Piper Warrior when we were interviewed for the position at Aputula in the Northern Territory and there were a few trips out to Arnhem Land. Otherwise all other flying was in the usual soulless commercial airlines.

Jandakot Airport - Royal Aero Club of WA.

Having moved from Darwin to Perth there came an opportunity to learn to fly. My three daughters had 'flown' the nest or were preparing to make their own way in life.

I signed up with the Perth Royal Aero Club at Jandakot Airport and my initial instructor was Amy Boulter who took me up for my introductory flight in an aerobatic Cessna 152 and scared the s**t out of me. The second flight with Amy wasn't much better so we didn't really click. I requested a change of instructor and was given Tom Wally an amiable practical chap who took me successfully through to being a qualified pilot. In fairness I must say that Amy Boulter went on to become a very successful commercial pilot in a very short period so probably had a very successful career.

Like anything else when starting from scratch it was a bit daunting to say the least given the complexity of the Airport and flying itself. Just sorting out the runways was challenging.

Jandakot Airport.

Flight-specific information:

This airport has three runways:

06L/24R, 1,392 m × 30 m (4,567 ft × 98 ft)

06R/24L, 1,150 m × 18 m (3,773 ft × 59 ft)

12/30, 1,508 m × 30 m (4,948 ft × 98 ft)

So, if the wind is coming from 240° SW you land (into the wind) on runway 06 Right/Left as instructed by the ATC (Air Traffic Controller). If the wind is coming from 60° NE then you land from the other end, ie runway 24 Right/Left and so on.

All the while I was being instructed in flying I was studying my theory such as meteorology, navigation, aviation law, radio, human performance etc. The expectation was, that once I was successful in the practical aspects of flying then I would have passed my theory exams culminating in a qualification to be a pilot and so it was. After thirteen hours of instruction Tom Wally took me for the usual circuit exercises – take off, climb out, left turn crosswind then left turn again parallel with the airstrip levelling off at one thousand feet for down wind leg then a descending left turn onto the base leg turning finals at seven hundred feet monitoring the aircraft instruments while carrying out all the appropriate radio communications with the Air Traffic Controller (ATC) and if you are on a 'touch and go' exercise you land then while still moving put on full revs and away you go again. Well after Tom and I had done two circuits he asked my to go into the parking bay hopped out and to my surprise told me "It's about time you went solo if you are comfortable with that of course?" Of course I said I was comfortable (but nervous) so went out and did my first solo. Because it was a small plane having no instructor seated next to me it changed the weight flight characteristics so the C152 was a bit different to fly but I managed to do my first solo circuit the land all in one piece. I taxied back to the parking bay shut off the plane got out, tied it down and then walked back towards the Club House. Halfway to the Club House Tom came out and walked towards me "How did it go Max?" It took me a couple of seconds to wipe the smile off my face before I could answer. I had done it, flown an aeroplane on my own up to a thousand feet then successfully landed the damn thing and walked away with the plane available for further use. It was a good day.

"If you can walk away from a landing it was a good landing."

"If you can walk away from a landing and the plane can still be flown it was a bloody good landing."

Tom Wally & me after my first solo

ROYAL AERO CLUB
OF WESTERN AUSTRALIA (INC)

FIRST SOLO CERTIFICATE

This is to certify that

Max de Grussa

has successfully completed a
FIRST SOLO FLIGHT

with the
Royal Aero Club of Western Australia on

8th May 2001

INSTRUCTOR

PRESIDENT

CHIEF FLYING INSTRUCTOR

My first solo was only the start of further intensive training with numerous circuits, navigation, forced landings and so on. The training was quite rigorous and thorough which it has to be at this stage with the emphasis not only on being able to find your way around (navigation) but also learning the legal rules so to keep yourself and others safe. It was and had to be repetitive. Radio communication between aircraft and the Air Traffic Controller was relentless with a range of checkpoints and strict procedures for leaving and entering the airfield. I often wondered how these people (ATC) coped with a bunch of aeroplanes flying in and out and all over the place but there wasn't a major incident while I was there. Accidents were rare, mostly due to pilot error. Aircraft maintenance was tightly regulated with again, strict procedures

View of Jandakot Airfield while I'm doing a circuit on runway 06 left.

All through training there was an underlying emphasis of staying alive as there were forces out there just waiting to kill you including other aircraft but the main threat was gravity, a force to be reckoned with. Tom said to me "Gravity has one purpose and that is to force you to crash into the ground as fast and hard as possible. It wants to kill you."

With this always (to this day) in mind I continued with my training.

I did have an incident, when on one landing I applied the brakes to slow done and the left brake seize up unbeknown to me so when I let the brakes off the right brake came off and the left brake stayed on so I slewed off the runway between two landing lights (thankfully) and came to a stop in a sandy patch between the two runways, a bit shaken but not stirred. A mechanic came out to release the brake allowing me to move the aircraft to the maintenance hanger. All good, I survived.

Apart from the immediate Jandakot Airport area there was what they called the 'Training Area' roughly a 10 nautical mile circle south of Jandakot where I could learn skills like stalls and forced landings and a few other things to ensure that if something goes wrong I can get out of it keeping myself and passengers safe. While I could be solo in the immediate Jandakot Airport area I was unable to be solo in the training area until passed my General Flying Progress Test which in due course I did so was then set free to hone my skills in the training area.

This also includes being able to land at Murrayfield Aerodrome (owned by the Royal Aero Club) a small airfield some 50 kilometres (34 miles) south of Jandakot Airport. It had one asphalt runway (12/30) and one gravel runway however, I used this airfield infrequently.

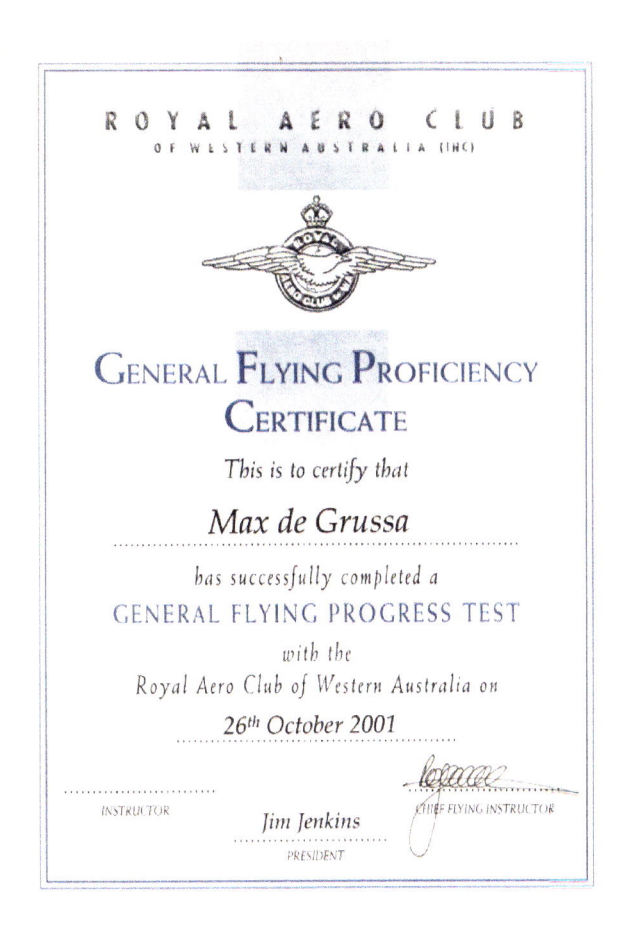

ROYAL AERO CLUB
OF WESTERN AUSTRALIA (INC)

GENERAL FLYING PROFICIENCY CERTIFICATE

This is to certify that

Max de Grussa

has successfully completed a
GENERAL FLYING PROGRESS TEST
with the
Royal Aero Club of Western Australia on
26th October 2001

INSTRUCTOR

Jim Jenkins
PRESIDENT

CHIEF FLYING INSTRUCTOR

Murrayfield Aerodrome checking all is clear from the air.

Landing at Murrayfield Aerodrome.

I did land a DHC-1 Chipmunk belonging to the Royal Aero Club at Murryfield on a training run but didn't continue training on this aircraft as I was spending more and more time in England for work. I thought a tail dragger might come in handy one day? The C in DHC-1 designated a Canadian built aircraft. Chipmunks replaced DH82 Tiger Moths as training aircraft in the Royal Australian Air Force.

DHC-1 Chipmunk VH-FLC

My daughter Angelique was my first passenger so a special occasion. As we are both adventurous sorts, not giving it any thought, we both just piled into the Cessna 152 and went for a couple of circuits.

Angie my first passenger

My second daughter Colette and her son Jared also were in the first few passengers in the dual seat Cessna 152.

My third daughter Jacqueline never did come flying with me!! Perhaps she was a very wise daughter?

Finally I was licensed:

SE Aeroplanes not exceeding 5,700 KG MTOW.

(Single Engine Aeroplanes not exceeding 5,700 kilograms maximum take off weight)

I puddled around with the two seat C152 for a while but then went for an endorsement to fly a four seat Cessna 172 (type conversion) the next step up as not only could I carry three passengers but it was a more sophisticated plane to fly.

Endorsement to fly Cessna 172
VH-BOF

Once endorsed, I puddled around between the C152 and the C172 mainly to get experience in between working and travelling to and from England.

My first passenger in the C172 was my daughter Angelique (again) but after that I had to spend most of time in England with decreasing infrequency time to fly in Australia.

Colette, Jacqueline nor anyone else offered nor badgered me to be a passenger thereafter as they were all getting on with their lives.

The majority of my flying would shift to the United Kingdom and Europe. The shift was brought about by work requirements as we were building a biodiesel refinery on an industrial site called Seal Sands near Middlesbrough northeast England. Initially we were based in London for approximately twelve months where the project's financial and business plans were fine tuned, then used for the basis of a prospectus on which to raise project funding. I missed family but in the end I would live permanently in the UK hoping to return.

I regularly visited my hometown of Perth, Western Australia and on one occasion accompanied my daughter Colette to Jandakot Airport where she went for a flight in a DH82 Tiger Moth.

Colette behind strut climbing onto the wing to get into the front cockpit.

All secured, the pilot taxis from the apron out to the runway for a flight over Perth city. By all accounts Colette enjoyed it immensely.

England - Teesside Airport

I settled near Middlesbrough, initially residing in Busby House on the outskirts of the lovely market town of Stokesley. Once settled in I looked around to find a suitable airfield to continue my flying. My first choice was the small airfield at Bagby near Thirsk some twenty miles (30k) from Stokesley. By this time I had moved from Busby House into Stokesley. It was on a cold crisp February day that I drove down to the Bagby airfield, a small grass strip with about thirty active aircraft and pilots. The guy who owned the airfield was an ex-Royal Airforce Pilot who at the time was entertaining some of his friends from the RAF which was an inebriated event. "Excuse me," I said, "I'm looking for an airfield to convert my Australian license to the British equivalent." He looked at me through bleary eyes and said "F**k off, we don't have antipodeans at this airfield." His mates erupted in a cacophony of laughter as I walked off. Leaving Bagby I drove to Teesside Airport where the reception was much more civilised. (Antipodeans are Australians or New Zealanders – a term used by people in northern hemisphere.)

This is Bagby Airfield coming into land on the west runway 24 (heading west 240°)

I would be back at Bagby in the not too distant future where I would hanger my Piper Super Cub and spent many a wonderful day with the new owners and fellow pilots.

Teesside Airport coming into land on Runway 05 (heading north 50°)

28

Teesside Airport was built during the WWII and was known as Goose Pool. I had (or have?) a book (Goose Pool) on its history.

As per aerodrome manual, quoted distances:
Runway 23 Take-off Run Available (TORA) – 2291m.
Runway 23 Take-off Distance Available (TODA) – 2488m.
Runway 05 Take-off Run Available (TORA) – 2291m.
Runway 05 Take-off Distance Available (TODA) – 2576m.

The runway is a massive 2291m and excellent to learn on. It's a full commercial airport.

There were several aero clubs based at the Teesside Airport so I went with the one with the café and the most sociable group of guys. Even though I was qualified in Australia I had to do several conversion courses especially in meteorology, as the climate was so different and aviation law, given that Australia is so sparse and England is so congested. In the end I repeated all of the theory and did the practical training more for confidence and safety.

Very soon I had my British JAR-PPL (Joint Aviation Requirements Flight Crew License – Private Pilot License)

My flying instructor was a guy called Dale Reynolds and I couldn't have wished for a better instructor, as he was a people person, caring and patient, not a bad bone in his body as they say. Everyone liked him and fortunately we became close friends and did quite a bit of flying together.

Flight Instructor Dale Reynolds.

While I was writing this I googled Dale and found he had died May 2021. It was a shock because I realised we have been out of touch for at least 3-4 years. I didn't really know how old Dale was although at a guess I'd put him 5 years older than me so in 2021 he could have been 77 if not older. He was a heavy smoker when I knew him and 2021 was peak Covid period when he died. I miss him.

Once I had passed all theory and practical requirements there was a graduation ceremony where each of us were presented with our 'Wings' as a symbol of being fully qualified pilots.

CLEVELAND FLYING SCHOOL
WINGS PRESENTATION 28 JANUARY 2006
DURHAM TEES VALLEY INTERNATIONAL AIRPORT
UNITED KINGDOM

(left to right)
Dr Trevor White (my aviation medical Dr)
Alan Wrigley (Chief Flying Instructor)
Max de Grussa Qualified JAR-FCL ie UK PPL (A) 7 December 2005
Dale Reynolds (my Flying Instructor)

From left to right (above):
Dr Trevor White who did all my medicals.

Alan Wrigley CFI (Chief Flying Instructor) who took all my flying examinations.

Max de Grussa (me) qualified British pilot.

Dale Reynolds a great instructor & friend RIP.

The flying community is quite large or was until the costs of flying became inhibiting, when I started all was affordable and we had so much fun.

LESLEY CHARLTON & MAX DE GRUSSA
MAY 30, 2005
JET PROVOST MK3A BASED AT NEWCASTLE AIRPORT (EGNT) UK
PILOT: NEIL MCCARTHY

(above) Lesley II and I being Jet pilots, great day. In a dive from 10k feet (3k meters) levelling out at 2k feet (610 meters) we reached a speed of 420 kts/h or 483 m/ph or 778 km/h – very exciting.

MAX DE GRUSSA & DALE REYNOLDS
JULY 10, 2005 RAF BULLDOG C120 G-CBBT
DURHAM TEES VALLEY (EGNV) TO RAF CRANWELL (EGYD)
PILOT: MAX DE GRUSSA

The above flight with Dale was into RAF Cranwell one of the oldest airfields in the UK. My friend

Bob Jackson was a Wing Commander there and we flew together often. He and his wife Karen were very close friends of Lesley and mine so we spent much time at this military base.

Some of the other planes I flew were: Cessna 150, 152,172,180 & 206; Piper PA28, PA34 & PA38; Diamond DA40; Grummand AA5; Yakovlev YAK 52; WWII Lancaster bomber; Jet Provost; Spitfire; Grob; Technam P2002; Airtourer; de Havilland DH82a Tiger Moth: L39 Albatross Russian jet trainer; Mustang P51: Robinson R22 & R44 helicopters; Scottish Aviation Bulldog Series 120; Beach Baron Twin; Slingsby T67M; Piper Mooney M20; Aquila A210; Boeing-Stearman 75; Jet Ranger helicopter; EV97 Eurostar; Beagle Pup Series-1; Extra 200; DHC-1 Chipmunk

Also had the opportunity to have a taxi run in the WWII Lancaster NX611 'Just Jane' at an old WWII RAF base at a place called East Kirby south east of Middlesbrough near Lincoln. This was a very special experience as was my flight in a Jet Provost from Newcastle. The greatest experience was going for a flight in a WWII Supermarine T9 Spitfire PT462 SWA out of Fishburn airfield. The L39 Albatross Russian jet trainer, Mustang P51 and the DH82a Tiger Moth were all flying experience while on holiday in New Zealand

Apart from owning my own Piper Super Cub PA-18 I also had a 20% ownership of a Scottish Aviation Bulldog Series 120 and a Cessna 172. Although part ownership of an aircraft was a pain fraught with squabbles and difficulties as there was always the one or two members who didn't clean the aircraft after use or damaged it in someway and didn't report it etc. I soon left these groups and kept to my own Piper Super Cub at Bagby Airfield in which I had many hours of fun. (see the back of this book for plane details)

Bagby Airfield

After my initial 'run in' with the arrogant owner I kept away and based myself at the clubrooms at Teesside Airport. Then heard that the owner sold the airfield so went down to check it out as I had arranged to ship my Piper Super Cub from WA so needed a hanger for her. Bagby was perfect and there was available space in the hanger. So this became my new base with a group of like-minded private pilots, made many new friends and had a great few years there. The Piper Cub was shipped in a container from Jandakot Airport in Western Australia to Rotterdam in the Netherlands (Holland) then trans-shipped to Teesport, Middlesbrough. From there it was trucked to Bagby Airfield where we unloaded it in bits, then the container was loaded onto the truck and gone within three hours. It took one of the aeronautical engineers a couple of days to put it back together. That is, put the wings back on, propeller etc. given a test run and she was ready to be flown. An experienced pilot Tom Cassells volunteered to be the test pilot and as history shows all went well so she was mine to fly from then on.

I kept the Australian registration VH-JVL, which confused air traffic controllers and aviators no end. I was amazed at how many people didn't know the VH registration, for some reason most guessing it was a Netherlands registration!

I just loved flying VH (her) as she was a docile and safe plane.

Before VH, I would take every opportunity to fly which meant cadging a ride when and wherever I could. All over the United Kingdom, north to south, east to west, so many WWII airfields.

Piper Aircraft Corp PA-18; Reg: Australian VH-JVL; Serial Number: 18-6038
OWNER: Max de Grussa
Bought it in W/Australia 2006 and shipped it to
Bagby Airfield, Thirsk UK Oct 2007.
Sold December 2008

This is my Piper Super Cub PA-18 after she had been re-constructed from her trip from Australia. She was a dream to fly, not too fast and easy to land even though she was a tail dragger.

The Piper PA-18 Super Cub is a two-seat, single-engine monoplane. Introduced in 1949 by Piper Aircraft, it was developed from the PA-11 Cub Special, and traces its lineage back through the J-3 Cub to the Taylor E-2 Cub of the 1930s. In close to 40 years of production, over 10,000 were built.
Ref: Wikipedia

Born 1949 the PA-18 was one year younger than me!
I flew her everywhere mostly on my own as I appreciate my own space. Private pilots are difficult breed at the best of times because the very nature of a person wanting to become a pilot requires a high degree of independent thinking. We need to be in charge and rarely trust anyone else flying an aeroplane we are sitting in.
Summer in England can be a delightful season with sunshine sixteen hours a day, barmy days and evenings with good vision perfect for VFR (visual flight rules) flying. That is, if its not raining!! I remember one year when it rained all summer, so not much flying.

Flying down to Breighton Airfield was a favourite as it was a Second World War heavy bomber base and cold-war nuclear missile launch site but is now home to the historic aircraft collection of the **Real Aeroplane Company** and the **Real Aeroplane Club**, an active flying club whose members own and operate many unusual, classic and ex-military aircraft. They have a great clubhouse that make the best bacon sandwiches. Sunday mornings several of us would fly down and have a bacon sandwich while checking out the vintage planes. It was refereed to as the £150 bacon butty but all good fun. Flew to White Waltham near London, Fife in Scotland and many other places.

Breighton Airfield (ex-RAF Breighton WWII)

(Max de Grussa (me) 3rd from the left)

A few of us flew down to RAF Scampton where we met the RAF Red Arrows 'Top Gun' pilots and a great bunch of chaps they were. RAF Scampton is where No. 617 Squadron was based WWII commonly known as "The Dambusters".

MAX DE GRUSSA

MUSTANG P51D – PILOT: ROBERT BORRIUS BOEK (ZK-SAS)
JANUARY 05, 2006 OMAKA NEW ZEALAND

L39C ALBATROSS – PILOT: ROBERT BORRIUS BOEK (ZK-WLM)
JANUARY 06, 2006 OMAKA NEW ZEALAND

TIGER MOTH DH82a – PILOT: S SOUTHAM (ZK-BFH)
JANUARY 10, 2006 OLD MANDAVILLE AIRFIELD NEW ZEALAND

Lesley II and myself had a wonderful holiday in New Zealand touring the north and south islands.
I flew (2nd in command) the Mustang P51D (Omaka), L39C Albatross (Omaka) and the Tiger Moth DH82a (Old Mandaville Airfield)

Cessna 172. Reg: G-AVVC
Originally based at Durham Tees Valley Airport then Bagby Airfield, Thirsk in 2008
M de Grussa was one of the original group of eight who owned and flew G-AVVC

G-YYAK owned by J Armstrong & D Lamb @ DTV Airport
M de Grussa B/Seat (P2) flew on 14th May 2006 (1 hr)

I owned 1/8th share in the Cessna 172 and loved flying it as a very safe plane plus would take four of us on a day out.

The YAK52 was a Russian Air Force trainer, a very well built hardy aircraft and great to fly – a one off very exciting flight.

MAX DE GRUSSA
SEPTEMBER 24, 2005
VICKERS SUPERMARINE LTD SPITFIRE MK.T IX (MODIFIED) G-CTIX
1 x PACKARD MOTOR CAR CO MERLIN 224
PILOT: ANTHONY HODGSON

Built for the R.A.F in 1944 at the famous Castle Bromwich works near Birmingham, PT462 started life as a single seat H.F Mk IX. It was delivered to 39 MU on 21st July 1944 being dispatched by sea on 9th August to the Mediterranean Allied Air Force based in Italy. It was known to have served with 253 Squadron coded as SW-A and is thought to have been used by 4 Squadron South African Air Force in the Mediterranean area as well.

Most exciting flight ever, in this iconic aeroplane. Once we were at 500 feet I was given control and took her to 7k feet where I did wing overs, loops, barrel rolls etc to get the feel of what it was like in a dog fight WWII. About 400 kt/ph (741 km/ph) it was fast and furious with the Packard Merlin 244 engine putting out 1.340 HP!!

43

Slingsby T67M Firefly Mk2 . Reg: G-BVLI
Based at Durham Tees Valley Airport
M de Grussa flew it 5th August 2006 (1hr)

G-BKWY owned by Cleveland Flying School
Durham Tees Valley Airport
M de Grussa flew regularly 2005 and 2006

The Slingsby T67M is a fully aerobatic plane owned by Tom Cassells (instructor) so I did many hours aerobatic training which was the best fun throwing the aircraft around loops, wing overs, vertical stalls, Immelmann turns, spin etc.
G-BKWY is a Cessna 150 trainer.

Cessna 172R . Reg: G-OPFT
Based at Durham Tees Valley Airport
M de Grussa regular flying for GA (Thruxton), night flying training
and some IMC training 2006/2007

G-BPKM PIPER PA-28-161 CHEROKEE WARRIOR II @ DTV Airport
M de Grussa flew several times 2007 for IMC training

The Cessna 172R was well equipped with partial glass cockpit and autopilot. Myself, Lesley, Dale & Margaret flew down to Thruxton racing circuit for a weekend where Dale and I did a racecar course. The PA-28 Cherokee was used learning IMC (Instrument Meteorological Conditions)

Robinson R22 – I had 22 hours of flight instruction on this helicopter but decided to stick with fixed wing aircraft so discontinued instruction.

Had a on-off flight in a Robinson R44 the big brother to the R22. Easier to fly four seats rather than two!

Also had a one-off flight in a jet ranger similar to this one, a different level of flying to the Robinson helicopters.

My flight patch

There is a story behind this patch as the guys at the Teesside Flying Club called me dog one. The reason is that my wife Lesley had a poodle called Sophie and the first time I asked her to come flying with me she brought Sophie along. I was unaware that I was not allowed to take a dog into the secured airside, that is, through the gate into the area where the planes are parked up or into the hangar.

A zealous new warden spotted the poodle and in a clandestine fashion took some photos of the offensive terrorist. I was issued with an official notice for breach of rules and banned from airside for three months much to the hysterical joy of my fellow pilots. Thus I acquired the nickname dog one and they issued the flight patch for my flight suit.

Confessions

There were a few of mishaps in my flying career, not many mind you but my daughter Angie and son-in-law Jason have "encouraged" me into confessing at least one of them. When my Piper Super Cub was based at Jandakot, Perth, Western Australia I took Jason for a fly on a bright but windy day. Even thought I had passed my endorsement to fly this tail dragger and was aware of the inherent danger of ground looping on landing I did exactly that. Once on the ground the plane aided by the wind spun around on the ground tipping the right wing so it hit the tarmac and then stopped. Normally the pilot would correct such a danger by rigorously working the rudder to compensate but obviously I didn't apply enough rudder to compensate. There was only slight damage to the wing tip and Jason and I walked away unscathed although Jason was a bit shaken!

The only other mishap was at Bagby Airfield when taking off in the Cub on 06 with a right crosswind, as I left the ground a sudden gust of wind slewed the plane left giving me a heading straight for the windsock pole. Fortunately I banked sharply to the right avoiding the pole by a few feet, straightened up and went on my merry way.

A couple of friends called me "STUKA" because I would often come into land high and side slip in or just dive in if on a long approach. All good.

AIRFIELDS FLOWN FROM/TO:

Western Australia	Ireland Republic
Perth	Galway
Jandokot	
Murrayfield	**New Zealand**
Bunbury	Omaka Blenhiem
Albany	Wanaka
Ballidu	Mandeville
Rottnest Island	
Dale River	**France**
	Toulouse (Las Bordes)
England	
Durham Tees Valley	**Austria**
Gampston (Retford)	Wein Neustadt
RAF Scampton	
White Waltham	
Leeds	
RAF Cranwell	
Fishburn	
RAF Leeming	
Elvington	
Sandtoft	
Tollerton (Nottingham)	
Breighton	
Full Sutton	
Beverley	
Sturgate	
Fadmoor	
Kirbymoorside	
Eshott	
Carlisle	
Newcastle	
Sherburne	
Felix Kirk	
Edds Field	
Sutton Bank	
Coventry	
Bagby	
Wycombe Air Park	
Thruxton	
Fenland	
Little Gramsden	

Aircraft Description

The following aircraft are ones that I had been endorsed to fly or aircraft that I had not been endorsed to fly but a second pilot. That is I supported the pilot through navigation, radio or general management while flying. This was often the case when I was the pilot in charge and had a fellow pilot with me. The other situation was where I was the pilot with an instructor receiving some particular training.

To make it easier to understand which was which I have colour coded the names of the aircraft:

Endorsed to fly = Blue (Pilot in charge)

Second pilot = Red

Pilot in training = Brown

Flying experience = Black

The point here is that I would jump at the chance to get into any plane I hadn't flown and if I wasn't invited I would invite myself. I couldn't get enough of flying or being associated with flying and only wish I could have made a career out of aviation but that was not to be of course.

Cessna 150 (flew from Teesside)

Role	Light utility aircraft, Basic trainer
National origin	United States
Manufacturer	Cessna
First flight	September 12, 1957
Produced	1958–1977
Number built	23,839

Cessna 152 (flew from Jandakot, WA)

Role	Basic trainer,
National origin	United States
Manufacturer	Cessna
Introduction	1977
Produced	1977–1985
Number built	7,584

Cessna 172 (Bagby & Teesside, UK)

Role	Civil utility aircraft
National origin	United States
Manufacturer	Cessna Textron Aviation
Introduction	1956
Produced	1956–1986, 1996–present
Number built	44,000+

Cessna 180 SkyWagon (Jandakot, WA)

Role	Light utility aircraft
National origin	United States
Manufacturer	Cessna
First flight	May 26, 1952
Introduction	1953
Produced	1953–1981
Number built	6,193

Cessna 206 (Darwin. Australia)

Role	Light aircraft
Manufacturer	Cessna
Introduction	1962 (206)
Status	In production
Produced	1962–1986 and 1998–present
Number built	over 8509 (as of approx. 2006)

Cessna 310 (Darwin, Australia)

Role	Twin-engine cabin monoplane
Manufacturer	Cessna
First flight	January 3, 1953
Introduction	1954
Primary user	United States Air Force
Produced	1954–1980
Number built	5,449 (310) 577 (320)

Piper PA-18 Super Cub (Owner: VH-JVL Bagby, UK)

Role	Light utility aircraft
National origin	United States
Manufacturer	Piper Aircraft
Introduction	1949
Produced	1949–1983/1988–1994
Number built	10,326

Piper PA-28-180 Cherokee (Teesside, UK)

Role	Civil utility aircraft
National origin	United States
Manufacturer	Piper Aircraft
First flight	14 January 1960
Introduction	1960
Produced	1961–present
Number built	32,778+

Piper PA-34-220T Seneca (Twin training) (Teesside to Galway, Republic of Ireland)

Role	Business and personal aircraft
National origin	United States
Manufacturer	Piper Aircraft
First flight	25 April 1967[2]
Introduction	1971
Produced	1971–present
Number built	5037 (until 2019)

Piper PA38 Tomahawk (flew from Bagby)

Role	Light aircraft
National origin	United States
Manufacturer	Piper
Introduction	1978
Produced	1978–1982
Number built	2,484

Diamond DA40 Diamond Star (Endorsement) (Teesside UK)

Role	Light aircraft
National origin	Austria
Manufacturer	Diamond Aircraft Industries
First flight	5 November 1997
Status	In production
Produced	1997–present
Number built	2,200 (December 2020)

Diamond DA 62 (Twin training)
(Wiener Neustadt, Austria)

Role	Twin engine light aircraft
National origin	Austria
Manufacturer	Diamond Aircraft Industries Aeromot
Introduction	October 2015
Produced	2015-present
Number built	120 (April 2019)
Developed from	Diamond DA50

Grumman AA5 (Bagby, UK)

Role	Four-seat cabin monoplane
National origin	United States
Manufacturer	American Aviation Grumman American Gulfstream American American General Aviation Corporation Tiger Aircraft
Produced	1971–2006
Number built	3,282

Yakovlev YAK 52 (Teesside UK)

Role	Two-seat trainer aircraft
National origin	Russia
Manufacturer	Yakovlev Aerostar
Introduction	1979
Primary users	Soviet Air Force DOSAAF
Produced	1978–1998

Lancaster (taxi run @ East Kirby)

Role	Heavy bomber
National origin	United Kingdom
Manufacturer	Avro
Introduction	February 1942
Primary users	Royal Air Force Canadian Air Force Australian Air Force
Number built	7,377

Jet Provost T5 (Newcastle UK)

Role	Military trainer aircraft
National origin	United Kingdom
First flight	26 June 1954
Introduction	1955
Retired	1993
Primary user	Royal Air Force
Produced	1958–1967
Number built	734

Spitfire (I flew it for 40 minutes – rear seat) (Sedgefield UK)

Role	Fighter / Interceptor aircraft
National origin	United Kingdom
Manufacturer	Supermarine
Designer	R. J. Mitchell
Introduction	4 August 1938[1]
Primary users	Royal Air Force Canadian Air Force Free French Air Force USArmy Air Force
Number built	20,351

Grob 115 (Tutor) (Endorsement) (RAF Cranwell UK)

Role	Basic trainer
National origin	Germany
Manufacturer	Grob Aircraft
Introduction	1999
Primary users	Royal Air Force Egyptian Air Force Finnish Air Force Royal Navy Army Air Corps (UK)
Produced	1985–present

Technam P2002 (Mountain Skills NZ)

Role	Two-seat light single
National origin	Italy
Manufacturer	Tecnam

AESL Airtourer 100/A1 (Mountain skills NZ)

Role	Light utility aircraft
National origin	Australia
Manufacturer	Victa Ltd
Introduction	1962 (100) 1963 (115)
Produced	1962–1966 (100 and 115, Victa) 1967–1973 (115 and 150, AESL)
Number built	168 (Aust); 80 (NZ)

DH82a Tiger Moth (Mandiville NZ)

Role	Trainer
National origin	United Kingdom
Manufacturer	de Havilland Aircraft Company de Havilland Canada
Designer	Geoffrey de Havilland
Introduction	February 1932
Number built	8,868

L39 Albatross (Russian jet trainer NZ)

Role	Military trainer
National origin	Czechoslovakia
Manufacturer	Aero Vodochody
Introduction	28 March 1972 with the Czechoslovak Air Force[2]
Primary users	Soviet Air Force Czechoslovak Air/F
Produced	1971–1996/2023 -
Number built	2,900

Mustang P51 (NZ flight)

Role	Fighter
National origin	United States
Manufacturer	North American Aviation
Introduction	January 1942 (RAF)[2]
Primary users	US Army Air Forces Royal Air Force NZ Air Force Canadian Air Force
Number built	More than 15,000[4]

Robinson R22 (24 hours training Teesside)

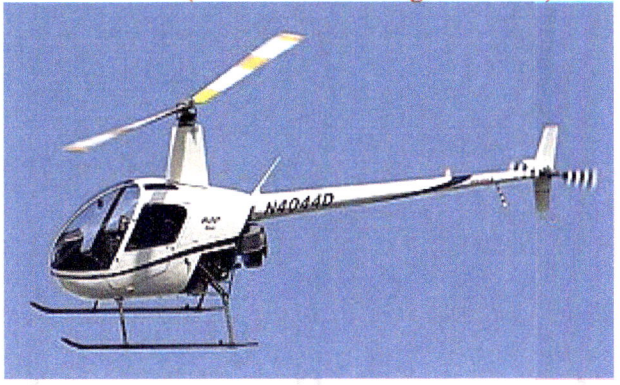

Role	Light utility and trainer helicopter
National origin	United States
Manufacturer	Robinson Helicopter Company
Introduction	1979
Status	In production[1]
Produced	1979–present
Number built	over 4,600 (2015)

Robinson R44 (Teesside Airport, UK)

Role	Light utility and trainer helicopter
National origin	United States
Manufacturer	Robinson Helicopter Company
First flight	31 March 1990
Introduction	1993
Produced	1990–present
Number built	6,331+ (through 2019)

Scottish Aviation - Bulldog Series 120 (Flew from Sedgefield UK)

Role	Basic trainer with aerobatic capability
Manufacturer	Beagle Aircraft/Scottish Aviation
First flight	19 May 1969
Introduction	1971
Status	Active
Primary user	Royal Air Force
Produced	1969–1982
Number built	328

Beach Baron 58P (Jandakot, Perth, WA)

Role	Civil utility aircraft
National origin	United States
Manufacturer	Beechcraft
First flight	February 29, 1960 [1]
Primary user	United States Army (historical)
Produced	1961–present
Number built	6,884+

Slingsby T67M (flew from Bagby)

Role	Trainer/tourer/sport aircraft
Manufacturer	Fournier [fr] Slingsby Aviation
First flight	12 March 1974
Retired	United States Air Force 2006
Primary users	Royal Jordanian Air Force Belize Defence Force Air Wing Bahrain Air Force
Produced	1974–1995
Number built	> 250

Mooney M20J (Jandakot, Perth, WA)

Role	Personal use civil aircraft
Manufacturer	Mooney International Corporation
Introduction	1955
Produced	1955–1971, 1974–2008, 2014–2019
Number built	>11,000

Aquila A 210 (Flew in Toulouse, France)

Role	Two seat light aircraft
National origin	Germany
Manufacturer	Aquila Aviation by Excellence
Introduction	2000
Primary user	Cameroon Air Force
Number built	120 by early 2011

Boeing-Stearman Model 75 (Jandakot, Perth)

Role	Biplane trainer
Manufacturer	Stearman Aircraft / Boeing
Introduction	1934
Number built	8,584 (includes model 70, 75 and 76)[l]

Bell 206 JetRanger (Bagby, England)

Role	Multipurpose utility helicopter
National origin	United States/Canada
Manufacturer	Bell Helicopter
Introduction	1967
Status	In service
Produced	1962–2017
Number built	7,300

84

EV97 Eurostar (flew from Bagby)

Role	Light Sport Aircraft
National origin	Czech Republic
Manufacturer	Evektor-Aerotechnik
Status	In production
Produced	1997–present

Beagle Pup Series-1 (flew from Bagby)

Role	General Aviation
Manufacturer	Beagle Aircraft Limited
Produced	1967–1970
Number built	175

DHC-1 Chipmunk (Jandakot, Perth, WA)

Role	Trainer
Manufacturer	de Havilland Canada
Introduction	1946
Status	In service civilian use
Primary users	Royal Air Force (historical) Royal Canadian Air Force (historical) Portuguese Air Force
Produced	1947–1956
Number built	1,284 (including Canadian, British, and Portuguese production)[1]

Printed in Great Britain
by Amazon